In Search of Contemporary Man

BY KENNETH HAMILTON

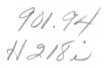
WILLIAM B. EERDMANS / PUBLISHER

FOR ALICE

CONTENTS

3

ACKNOWLEDGMENTS

This essay was originally written to be the opening program in a series of eight broadcasts given by the Canadian Broadcasting Corporation under the general title "The Human Condition." While it has been somewhat altered to fit the printed page, and some of the illustrative readings have been omitted and other pieces added, it remains substantially the same argument. I am much indebted to the producer of the program, Mr. Gerald Newman, and to the team of actors who interpreted the script over the air; and also to numerous correspondents who expressed the hope that the work might be made available in a written form. My thanks are due especially to Dr. Roderick Jellema, editor of the series "Contemporary Writers in Christian Perspective," for his encouragement and help at all stages of preparing the essay for publication. Although I must accept responsibility for the defects that remain, these would have been more numerous and more evident without his wise guidance and friendly counsel.

—K. H.

United College
Winnipeg

FOREWORD

I first encountered Kenneth Hamilton's *In Search of Contemporary Man* at what is now page twenty-six. It did not catch my eye, but my ear. On April 29, 1966 I was driving alone from the suburbs into Washington, D.C. At that time this superb little book was an unpublished radio script called *The Human Condition,* just then being broadcast in Canada by the Canadian Broadcasting Corporation. Although I have never before or since picked up the CBC in the before-midnight clutter of Washington's air waves, that night I accidentally did. Out of an unfamiliar crack between a dull ball game which the Senators were losing and one of those broadcast telephone arguments which nobody ever wins, a strong voice was saying,

> . . . . then our uncertainty and confusions today may actually be a source of strength. Even the absence of a universal religious framework for existence may prove to be a blessing in disguise. Though the other side of the medal is the danger of perishing through exposure to the cosmic cold of a pitiless sky as we shiver, like abandoned orphans, in the open field of the world. But men have usually managed to set up some kind of home even in the most unpropitious circumstances. . . .

As I drove farther down 16th Street the recreated drama of modern man intensified. The first voice was supplemented by other voices, voices reading words that burst like rockets in patterns traced and re-traced by the first voice's commentary — words by Nietzsche's Madman, Auden, Pascal, Proust, Eliot, Buber. When the station began fading behind the big downtown buildings, I parked, illegally, at a busy bus stop. A ticket could not have mattered in the least.

Anyone who heard that CBC broadcast must have been similarly moved. But I was the more excited because, as editor of a booklet series called *Contemporary Writers in Christian*

5

Perspective, I was searching, through books and periodicals and out into the blankness of the mails, for writers. I did not know who had conceived *The Human Condition,* selected its materials, unified it and threaded its brilliant commentary. But the author seemed to be a composite of all the writers real and imaginary that I had been thinking of; and his theological and literary insights were giving me a kind of overview of the series. I did not know until the sign-off that the author was Kenneth Hamilton.

That was the second oddity. I had never met Kenneth Hamilton, but I knew him well. I had read some articles of his on Beckett, Camus, Updike, and Salinger; we had been corresponding for a few months, and I had eagerly signed him to do *Salinger* and *Beckett* for the series. I had also just read his excellent critique of modern theology, *Revolt Against Heaven.* I knew him as a keen literary critic and as an exciting theologian — as a critic and theologian who kept the two sides of himself in enriching dialogue without letting them merge into some soft compound which is neither criticism nor theology. He is uniquely the man who could have created such a broadcast.

Now it is a book. What was meant to come in through the ear as *The Human Condition* has been revised to come in through the eye as *In Search of Contemporary Man.* It is a still more powerful weaving of essay and anthology, a still more powerful "interpretive survey," as Hamilton once called it.

For a few months we thought of the manuscript as a part of the *Contemporary Writers in Christian Perspective* series. It is too broad to fit that function. But reading it now, I feel as strongly as I ever have that it lights up the backdrop to the stage on which the series (and, indeed, modern literature) is performing. It clarifies the build-up of modern man's predicament — something which the individual booklets, in their concern with that predicament, cannot each do for themselves. It will prove an invaluable reference for all of the booklets in the series.

But this little book stands big by itself, too. Primarily it is

6

an encounter: an encounter with strong voices speaking clearly about the shaping and mis-shaping of the modern world, and an encounter with the steady, sympathetic voice of Kenneth Hamilton. The encounter ends, as Frost said a good poem ends, in clarification — in, at the very least, "a momentary stay against confusion."

—RODERICK JELLEMA

The University of Maryland
College Park

The Human Condition—20th Century Style

ONE OF THE LANDMARKS OF OUR AGE IS SAMUEL BECKETT'S play *Waiting for Godot*. A decade ago this play made a sensation in Paris, London and New York. Many walked out, finding it incomprehensible — or, maybe, not incomprehensible enough; at any rate, distasteful. But it made its impression and survived, to father a flock of other plays in the same mood and to become a recognized modern classic. It is neither the first nor the most shocking in the movement which we have come to know as "The Theatre of the Absurd." Yet in some ways it touches a sensitive spot in our consciousness more surely than the rest. It makes us turn to look at ourselves, not just individually but universally. We may try to shrug it off, to say that this world of *Waiting for Godot* is not our world, the world of the daily newspaper and the glossy magazine, of L.B.J. and the astronauts, of the Beatles and the Junior Chamber of Commerce. But we cannot altogether shut out the suspicion that, after all our denials, this world may nevertheless be exactly ours, and this our condition . . . the human condition. Beckett puts on his stage two hoboes, a young boy, a blustering egoist Pozzo who turns blind, and a miserable old man called Lucky, who carries a suitcase and a picnic basket and is driven around with a rope about his neck like an unmanageable horse. Like an unmanageable horse, he bites. Lucky turns dumb, but not before he has given his speech, which he does at Pozzo's word of command, "Think!"

9

SAMUEL BECKETT, Lucky's speech from Act I of *Waiting for Godot*, 1954

Given the existence as uttered forth in the public
works of Puncher and Wattmann of a personal
God quaquaquaqua with white beard
quaquaquaqua outside time without extension
who from the heights of divine apathia divine
athambia divine aphasia loves us dearly with
some exceptions for reasons unknown but time
will tell and suffers like the divine Miranda with
those who for reasons unknown but time will tell
are plunged in torment plunged in fire whose fire
flames if that continues and who can doubt it will
fire the firmament that is to say blast hell to
heaven so blue still and calm so calm with a calm
which even though intermittent is better than
nothing but not so fast and considering what is
more that as a result of the labors left unfinished
crowned by the Acacacacademy of
Anthropopopometry of Essy-in-Possy of Testew
and Cunard it is established beyond all doubt all
other doubt than that which clings to the labors
of men that as a result of the labors unfinished of
Testew and Cunard it is established as hereinafter
but not so fast for reasons unknown that as a
result of the public works of Puncher and
Wattmann it is established beyond all doubt that
in view of the labors of Fartov and Belcher left
unfinished for reasons unknown of Testew and
Cunard left unfinished it is established what many
deny that man in Possy of Testew and Cunard
that man in Essy that man in short that man in
brief in spite of the strides of alimentation and
defection wastes and pines wastes and pines and
concurrently simultaneously what is more for
reasons unknown in spite of the strides of physical
culture the practice of sports such as tennis
football running cycling swimming flying floating
riding gliding conating camogie skating tennis
of all kinds dying flying sports of all sorts autumn
summer winter winter tennis of all kinds hockey of
all sorts penicilline and succedanea in a word I
resume flying gliding golf over nine and eighteen
holes tennis of all sorts in a word for reasons

10

unknown in Feckham Peckham Fulham Clapham
namely concurrently simultaneously what is more
for reasons unknown but time will tell fades away
I resume Fulham Clapham in a word the dead
loss per head since the death of Bishop Berkeley
being to the tune of one inch four ounce per head
approximately by and large more or less to
the nearest decimal good measure round figures stark
naked in the stockinged feet in Connemara in a
word for reasons unknown no matter what matter
the facts are there and considering what is more
much more grave that in the light of the labors
lost of Steinweg and Peterman it appears what is
more much more grave that in the light the light
the light of the labors lost of Steinweg and
Peterman that in the plains in the mountains by
the seas by the rivers running water running fire
the air is the same and then the earth namely the
air and then the earth in the great cold the great
dark the air and the earth abode of stones in the
great cold alas alas in the year of their Lord six
hundred and something the air the earth the sea
the earth abode of stones in the great deeps the
great cold on sea on land and in the air I resume
for reasons unknown in spite of the tennis the
facts are there but time will tell I resume alas
alas on on in short in fine on on abode of stones
who can doubt it I resume but not so fast I
resume the skull fading fading fading
and concurrently simultaneously what is more for
reasons unknown in spite of the tennis on on the
beard the flames the tears the stones so blue so
calm alas alas on on the skull the skull the skull
the skull in Connemara in spite of the tennis the
labors abandoned left unfinished graver still
abode of stones in a word I resume alas alas
abandoned unfinished the skull the skull in
Connemara in spite of the tennis the skull alas the
stones Cunard tennis
. . . the stones . . . so calm . . . Cunard . . .
unfinished . . .

It is possible that this speech is offered as the sum total of
human knowledge to date. At least, that is one way of reacting

11

to it. The whole of what civilized man has learned and come to value, his art, his science, his philosophy, his religion, the worlds of politics and commerce and sport: all this may be reduced to a stream of impressively incoherent ranting. That is all. You have heard it.

Or most of it, at least. When Lucky gives his fractured précis of human knowledge, the others cannot bear it. They pull on the rope, try to drag him down, and finally take off his hat. He stops.

What is Lucky's précis? Is there anything in the end that man has to cling to when, crowned with his hat (the emblem of his dignity) and pulled about by a halter (the mark of his degradation), he finally is driven to think about the human condition? It is significant that the word of command he is given is "Think!" — not "Talk!" Presumably Lucky represents man as the intellectual in society, as his master represents man as power-seeker, organizer, ruler and success-story. The latter is a great eater.

Lucky's speech must be stripped of repetitions and jabber to see that it makes very good sense. Lucky shouts out, struggling with his tormentors:

> Given the existence/ of a personal God/ with a white beard/ outside time/ without extension/ who from the heights of divine apathia/ loves us dearly, with some exceptions for reasons unknown (but time will tell)/ and suffers with those/, who for reasons unknown (but time will tell)/, are plunged in torment/ in fire whose/ flames will fire the firmament/ that is to say/ blast hell to heaven, so blue, still and calm.

Lucky here conveys the contradictions of traditional Christian theology. Orthodox theology argues that God is outside time and impassible — but also personal and with human characteristics. God is supposed to love all, yet condemns some to hell fire. He is also supposed to suffer on behalf of sinners. Beckett speaks of the "divine Miranda," for Miranda in *The Tempest* says "O! I have suffer'd / With those that I saw suffer." God is like Shakespeare's heroine in the Christian belief that He suffers in His Son for fallen man. When we ask for reasons, we are told that we are in the presence of a divine mystery, which one day will be made clear to us. But Lucky suggests that, before men can believe this, hell will burn up heaven. And indeed, that is what happens when belief fades. Hell in us burns up heaven, depriving us of the peace which heaven symbolizes. How we would be glad of a little of that peace now, even if it came only intermittently! And believers looked forward to an eternity of heavenly calm! But false belief actually lets hell loose in man. Faith goes against experience.

Lucky then turns to consider, in an even more disjointed fashion, what is said to be *established beyond doubt* in other intellectual disciplines. "The Acacacacademy of Anthropopopometry" has "labors left unfinished." Philosophy can talk about what man may be, potentially, and this knowledge will be proclaimed by the pundits (Testew and Cunard, Fartov and Belcher — names made deliberately contemptuous in tone), coming to no conclusion in works that remain incomplete. Bishop Berkeley is dead. Philosophy is outmoded, and in Feckham, Peckham, Fulham and Clapham reasons are unknown. These place names suggest unfashionable, undistinguished districts in the great sprawl of London. In other words, the pure intellect does not speak to the modern, urban middle classes. All labor is lost, in spite of centuries of academic research. Anthropology, medicine, and the devotees of sport have no relevant word to say about man as he now exists. The ideal of a sane mind in a sane body is a dead ideal.

The irony of it all, as Lucky vainly tries to say as he is prevented from finishing, is that earth, air, fire and water — the world in its basic elements — remains constant. But all has grown cold and hard around us. We live on in an "abode of stones," "the skull fading, fading, fading." Man's labors to find meaning are lost labors. Intelligence is futile. The certainties of the past are gone, and with them the calm at the heart of life. Man is degraded, stripped of dignity, knowing in his inner self that he has something to say — even feeling

13

the compulsion to go on thinking in the face of every discouragement. But, in his terrors and anxieties, he has lost the power to communicate. The few scraps of wisdom he has left are not wanted. The intellect is pulled down, and the dignity of the intellectual is forcibly taken from him.

Is this, really, when the chips are down, what our culture, East and West, amounts to? Is the intellectual simply the misused and bitter slave of a materialistic society? Have the classical disciplines of the mind, along with religious faith, outlived their usefulness? When we land on the moon, will we have anything more to take there, after the wrappings of our splendid technological achievements are stripped off, than Lucky's suitcase and picnic basket and a few confused remnants of the wisdom of a dead past?

We have troubled consciences, you and I, or the Theatre of the Absurd would not touch a chord in us and set us vibrating uneasily. There is enough going on around us, surely, to keep us busy without a spare moment to think about ourselves. If we are inclined to think that the situation is exaggerated, nevertheless, we can hardly ignore the contradictions of our culture. We belong to the Affluent Society, yet poverty is still squatting within the gates at home and growing continually more menacing abroad. We pride ourselves, with due restraint of course, on our pragmatism — our ability to get things done and our coming at life with an open mind free from the dogmatisms of the past. Well, we need to keep reminding ourselves of all our up-to-the-minute know-how, and the vast variety of mechanical marvels we have learned to manipulate, before we can screw up enough courage to look the problems in the face that are facing us. New nations are springing up like dragons' teeth sown in the ground to rise as armed warriors. As if we had even begun to sort out the troubles of those we have already! And it will not help in the least for us to shout, "Stop the world, I want to get off." Statisticians tell us that our leaving a little early cannot affect the crisis caused by the numbers that are arriving. Mother Earth is in imminent danger of being trampled to death by her own children. The

14

cosmic horror-movie's sound track is nothing but the patter of little feet.

Yet we are more the pensive Hamlet than Fortinbras, the man of action. Having so much to do that calls out to be done without delay, we pause and look within. The problem that underlies our problems is Hamlet's: we have bad dreams. They are not just recent, either, these bad dreams. They have been with us as long as most of us can remember, anyway. The poets and the painters have been shouting at us to look, and pay attention to what is there, for a long, long time — way before the Theatre of the Absurd. The artist, whether his medium is verbal, pictorial, plastic, or musical, is the man equipped with radar to penetrate the cultural fogs of the age. Like the canaries that used to be taken down the mines or the white rabbits that once were carried aboard submarines, this race of mankind knows, before the rest, when the air is becoming poisonous or exhausted. And what the artists have given us is a series of variations upon one insistent theme; a cry that has steadily grown more shrill in each decade; a long lament over the loss of man's wholeness; and a running commentary on the stages of his disintegration. Lucky's speech ending with his description of the world as an "abode of stones" is an item in the inventory of the contemporary world, a list drawn up in the process of stocktaking in our intellectual storehouse.

After all, it was in 1922 that T. S. Eliot wrote *The Waste Land*.

T. S. ELIOT, *The Waste Land* (lines 19-24), 1922

What are the roots that clutch, what branches grow
Out of this stony rubbish? Son of man,
You cannot say, or guess, for you know only
A heap of broken images, where the sun beats,
And the dead tree gives no shelter, the cricket no relief,
And the dry stone no sound of water.

In that poem, too, as in Lucky's speech, there are caught up little pieces of the wisdom and beauty of the past. But Eliot's

15

universe is at an earlier stage of disintegration than the one which Beckett makes us glimpse through Lucky. Eliot still believes that it is possible to take the old universe of meaning that has been broken and refashion it into a new whole. As in the Bible the Psalmist turns in longing to God "in a dry and thirsty land where no water is," so Eliot turns to the literary classics of the cultural tradition in which he has been educated and quotes, now here, now there. "Against these fragments," he tells us in a famous phrase, he has "shored his ruins." Meaning is still to be found, though not easily; for it has to be pursued down tortuous paths strewn with many false clues. Finally, the poet's anguish is dissolved in the sound of the rain that is to bring fertility to the barren land.

Or one may compare Lucky's speech with a nearer parallel: the linguistic experiments of James Joyce. Beckett has close links with Joyce — closer even than the geographical link of Dublin, or the biographical link of being likewise an Irish expatriate living in France, or the intellectual link of having translated Joyce's *Anna Livia Plurabelle*. Yet, although he has gone to school in Joyce's workshop and has borrowed many of his tools, his apprenticeship has proved a springboard rather than a parking-place. Joyce discovered an aesthetic equivalent for the Catholic universe of his Jesuit schoolmasters. Both the interior monologue of the ending of *Ulysses* and the portmanteau-word dream language of *Finnegan's Wake* are incoherent only on the surface. Dive beneath, and a tightly knit structure is revealed. The apparently haphazard is designed, and the apparently confused is orderly. As in Joyce's words, so in the reality he discovers, nature and the human psyche are interlocked in a gigantic, intricate jigsaw puzzle, without a piece missing or a piece over. Whereas, Beckett's universe is like an effort to hold a cloud together with masking tape — futile, damp, sticky and comically frustrating.

Between the era of *Ulysses* and *The Waste Land* and the era of *Waiting for Godot* there lies the earnest Thirties. Then literature became politically conscious. In America the misery of the Depression was documented. In Europe the rise of totalitarianism was the imminent threat, and poets and novelists went to the wars in Spain and China. The frustrations of the era, and the cynicism bred by them, are caught in a poem Louis MacNeice wrote while in Scotland, seeing a stagnant economy wedded to a bankrupt morality.

LOUIS MACNEICE, "Bagpipe Music," 1938 (stanzas 2, 3, 6, 7)

John MacDonald found a corpse, put it under the sofa,
Waited till it came to life and hit it with a poker,
Sold its eyes for souvenirs, sold its blood for whiskey,
Kept its bones for dumbbells to use when he was fifty.

It's no go the Yogi-Man, it's no go Blavatsky,
All we want is a bank balance and a bit of skirt in a taxi.

Annie MacDougall went to milk, caught her foot in the heath-
er,
Woke to hear a dance record playing of Old Vienna.
It's no go your maidenheads, it's no go your culture,
All we want is a Dunlop tire and the devil mend the puncture.

It's no go the picture palace, it's no go the stadium,
It's no go the country cot with a pot of pink geraniums.
It's no go the Government grants, it's no go the elections,
Sit on your arse for fifty years and hang your hat on a
pension.

It's no go my honey love, it's no go my poppet;
Work your hands from day to day, the winds will blow the
profit.
The glass is falling hour by hour, the glass will fall forever,
But if you break the bloody glass you won't hold up the
weather.

Well, here we have a bit of a political tract, a Scots sermon somewhat in the tradition of John Knox, though scarcely in Presbyterian language — not that used in church, anyway. We can appreciate MacNeice's social message all the more because of our present acquaintance with that serious Social Gospeler, the folk singer, who has lately stepped into the vacant shoes of the Beat poet. But how deep does it go? Looking back with the advantage of hindsight, we may wonder whether the

real interest of MacNeice and his fellow bards of the Pink
Political Muse was not, in fact, the fragmented universe rather
than the collapsing economy, and man without direction rather
than man without a job. MacNeice's John MacDonald seems
to be at least a distant relative of Eliot's *Waste Land* character
Stetson, who also was involved with a corpse that wouldn't lie
down; and his Annie MacDougall a country cousin of the typist
in the same poem. Political concern or political indifference:
whichever way you go, it adds up to much the same in the
end for poetry. As Robert Frost contemplating the tree at his
window reminds us, the poet's awareness of the blowing of
the winds outside serves chiefly to quicken his reaction to inside weather.

ROBERT FROST, "Tree at My Window" in
West-Running Brook, 1928

Tree at my window, window tree,
My sash is lowered when night comes on;
But let there never be curtain drawn
Between you and me.

Vague dream-head lifted out of the ground
And thing next most diffuse to cloud,
Not all your light tongues talked aloud
Could be profound.

But tree, I have seen you taken and tossed,
And if you have seen me when I slept,
You have seen me when I was taken and swept
And all but lost.

That day she put our heads together,
Fate had her imagination about her,
Your head so much concerned with outer,
Mine with inner, weather.

Not for long is the human condition absent from the thoughts
of any responsible artist in this century, not even during the
Thirties. The distance from the city streets to the city of the
heart is never very far, anyway.

18

W. H. Auden, "Epilogue" from *Look, Stranger*, 1936

Certainly our city — with the byres of poverty down to
The river's edge, the cathedral, the engines, the dogs;
    Here is the cosmopolitan cooking
    And the light alloys and the glass.

Built by the conscious-stricken, the weapon-making,
By us. The rumours woo and terrify the crowd,
    Woo us. The betrayers thunder at, blackmail
    Us. But where now are They

Who without reproaches shewed us what our vanity has
    chosen,
Who pursued understanding with patience like a sex,
    had unlearnt
    Our hatred, and towards the really better
    World had turned their face?

There was Nansen in the north, in the hot south Schweitzer,
    and the neat man
To their east who ordered Gorki to be electrified;
    There were Freud and Groddeck at their candid
    studies
    Of the mind and body of man.

Nor was every author both a comforter and a liar;
Lawrence revealed the sensations hidden by shame,
    The sense of guilt was recorded by Kafka,
    There was Proust on the self-regard.

Who knows? The peaked and violent faces are exalted,
The feverish prejudiced lives do not care, and lost
    Their voice in the flutter of bunting, the glittering,
    Brass of the great retreat,

And the malice of death. For the wicked card is dealt, and
The sinister tall-hatted botanist stoops at the spring
    With his insignificant phial, and looses
    The plague on the ignorant town.

Under their shadows the pitiful subalterns are sleeping;
The moon is usual; the necessary lovers touch:
    The river is alone and the trampled flower,
    And through years of absolute cold

19

The planets rush towards Lyra in the lion's charge. Can
Hate so securely bind? Are They dead here? Yes.
    And the wish to wound has the power. And tomorrow
    Comes. It's a world. It's a way.

That is not vintage Auden, perhaps, but it is quite representative of W. H. Auden's outlook in the mid-Thirties. It follows a traditional pattern, that of the "Ubi Sunt?" (or "Where-Are-They?") poem, lamenting present ills and looking back to the great men who once inspired us — a "Milton, thou shouldst be living at this hour" sort of thing.

Auden sees the city of civilization doomed because of apathy, prejudice and ignorance. At this time his faith is centered to a large extent in psychology, by means of which he believes man can be remade, individually and socially. So his heroes are chiefly psychologists of one sort or another. They are either the great scientific figures in the field of human behavior — Freud and Groddeck — or else they are the literary, intuitive psychologists — Proust, Kafka and Lawrence. "If only people would learn!" Auden complains, " — but our vanity has made us choose to stay with our hatred and guilt, turning our backs on those who could save us."

Auden has men of action for heroes also. But they are also pioneers in extending the ability of man to understand himself. Their actions are on the frontiers of the outer world as the psychologist's work is on the frontiers of the inner one. Nansen's explorations in the arctic wastes are not unlike Freud's explorations in the human unconscious.

Albert Schweitzer is counted by Auden among those — "where now are They" — who "had unlearnt our hatred, and towards the really better/World had turned their faces." Since Schweitzer went to his work of healing "in the hot south" from religious convictions, we may ask where religion fits into the twentieth-century concern with the human condition.

Our age is characterized by secularism, because secularism is the ideological expression of technology. And the civilization in which we live is — whatever else it may be — a technological civilization. If an individual professes a religion today, it is because he personally decides to do so, and not because the surrounding culture demands it. Artists, like other members of the community, are a mixed bunch: of believers of different persuasions, non-believers and non-attached agnostics. Maybe on account of their concern with the human condition they wrestle with the question of religion more than other groups. Auden, for example, came to shift his interests from the psychological to the spiritual dimension of man's being. Like Eliot before him, he moved over to an explicitly Christian reading of human life and destiny.

It is not surprising that concentration upon the human condition should lead some artists to find religion a live option as they explore the landscape of the human self. The religious vision is one answer to the riddle of human existence; and it is an answer that declares itself right at the center of man's descent into himself, when the resources of self-analysis are exhausted. Then comes the decision to accept — or not to accept — an understanding of the self and the world going beyond the bounds of the available and the verifiable. The religious believer says that not to believe would be a denial of the truth that has flashed upon his life, a truth establishing itself beyond his experience, yet confirming all other truths that he has discovered in his experience. The sceptic, choosing the opposite road, says that to believe is to take the easy way out. And the easy way is also the dishonest way. It is to demand the abdication of reason, so that we may live in the false security of a universe patterned after our wishes and not according to reality.

The debate continues, and no impartial arbitration is possible. Yet, on whichever side he happens to stand, and wherever he has found his final loyalty, the artist helps us to see what is involved in making a decision. Most surely, if he cannot accept some religious consolation, and if the universe brings no healing pattern to his human understanding, the artist will not let us sit down comfortably in our easy chairs, cushioned against the promptings of inner discontent. This is when Beckett sends Lucky to shout in our ears. And, not only for our sakes but also for his own, the artist cannot rest until he has found his way to some equilibrium, however precarious, among those forces threatening our selfhood, forces which he feels easily enough, even if we do not. Sometimes he has little to advise except some "style" of living, an attitude to adopt in order to preserve some values for mankind in spite of the inevitable advance of the tide of chaos and the dissolution of tradition; and sometimes he comes with a meticulously worked-out metaphysic of existence, showing by illustration how it can be applied to the concrete situations of life. (E. M. Forster and Thomas Mann, for example, seem to fall into the first category and Jean-Paul Sartre into the second.) Yet, the more deeply he feels the absence of the healing power of a common religious vision, the more the artist is likely to look expectantly and longingly for some new revelation to banish our perplexities. By bringing an undeniable presence into the void of a meaningless universe, religion will once again, as in the past, kindle the light of the human spirit. Though what form this presence will take we cannot foresee; we can see only its power.

Such, in fact, was the dream that W. B. Yeats entertained, long before *meaninglessness* had become a common problem to discuss, and even before Eliot's *The Waste Land* had been published. In his poem "The Second Coming" he balances the two themes: present formlessness and the coming of a new order, born of mystery and so frightening to contemplate.

W. B. YEATS, "The Second Coming," 1920-21

Turning and turning in the widening gyre
The falcon cannot hear the falconer;
Things fall apart; the centre cannot hold;
Mere anarchy is loosed upon the world,
The blood-dimmed tide is loosed, and everywhere
The ceremony of innocence is drowned;
The best lack all conviction, while the worst
Are full of passionate intensity.

Surely some revelation is at hand;
Surely the Second Coming is at hand.
The Second Coming! Hardly are those words out

When a vast image out of *Spiritus Mundi*
Troubles my sight: somewhere in sands of the desert
A shape with lion body and the head of a man,
A gaze blank and pitiless as the sun,
Is moving its slow thighs, while all about it
Reel shadows of the indignant desert birds.
The darkness drops again; but now I know
That twenty centuries of stony sleep
Were vexed to nightmare by a rocking cradle,
And what rough beast, its hour come round at last,
Slouches towards Bethlehem to be born?

II

The Lonely "I"

THE NEW REVELATION OF WHICH YEATS DREAMED DID NOT arrive, but instead "the blood-dimmed tide" continued to flow, and its waters spread wider and wider. For some in Germany, for a time, anarchy was halted and a new revelation given in the will of Adolf Hitler. There were German philosophers — Martin Heidegger among them — who found in the Führer, as the decisive embodiment of the Nazi revolution, a new reality and an absolute standard of values. So perhaps Yeats's prophecy was partly fulfilled in a negative fashion, with an all-too-literal "rough beast." For Yeats had believed it possible that the universe might be turning back to its beginnings in primal chaos.

At any rate, there is no harm done in remembering that religions may be dark and demonic, and that a return to religion is not necessarily a victory for sweetness and light. We know that a dark religion can be powerful in its hold over men's imaginations. Yet, short of a universal relapse into barbarism, we shall not take this road. So we remain with our problem of the human self and with our inability to relate man to his world with confidence and in wholeness.

It may be that our problem is not wholly that of religion but one which, in the history of mankind, has been closely bound up with religion, namely, an imaginative picture of the universe in which we find ourselves and come to know ourselves. This truth has been explored quite remarkably by the great modern Jewish philosopher and religious thinker Martin Buber. In an essay with the title "What Is Man?" Buber explains how we do not stop to ask the question of the human condition unless we first feel ourselves lonely and uncertain of ourselves.

MARTIN BUBER, from "What Is Man?" in *Between Man and Man,* 1947

> The man who feels himself solitary is the most readily disposed and most readily fitted for the self-reflection of which I am speaking; that is, the man who by nature or destiny or both is alone with himself and his problematic, and who succeeds, in this blank solitude, in meeting himself, in discovering man in his own self, and the human problematic in his own. The times of spiritual history in which anthropological thought has so far found its depth of experience have been those very times in which a feeling of strict and inescapable solitude took possession of man; and it was the most solitary men in whom the thought became fruitful. In the ice of solitude man becomes most inexorably a question to himself, and just because the question pitilessly summons and draws into play his most secret life he becomes an experience to himself.
>
> In the history of the human spirit I distinguish between epochs of habitation and epochs of homelessness. In the former, man lives in the world as in a house, as in a home. In the latter, man lives in the world as in an open field and at times does not even have four pegs with which to set up a tent. In the former epochs anthropological thought exists only as a part of cosmological thought. In the latter, anthropological thought gains depth and, with it, independence.

If Buber is correct, or at all on the mark, then our uncertainty and confusions today may actually be a source of strength. Even the absence of a universal religious framework for existence may prove to be a blessing in disguise. Though the other side of the medal is the danger of perishing through exposure to the cosmic cold of a pitiless sky as we shiver, like abandoned orphans, in the open field of the world. But men have usually managed to set up some kind of a home even in the most unpropitious circumstances; and, once they have settled in, they often have refused to move even when better accommodation was available. Perhaps this applies to us, too, in our intellectual refugee-camp existence.

Buber's argument that cosmological thought alternates with anthropological thought is a fascinating one. Without trying to follow it through in the way he does, it is worth looking at a few instances of how it works out, because the two ways of understanding reality are present in our own everyday thinking, whether or not we ever stop to disentangle them.

The cosmological view finds its purest expression in the world view of Aristotle, with its picture of the universe as concentric spheres having our earth at the center. As Buber points out, the picture is wholly *visual*. This is a universe we see. Like the tidy world which our grandmothers wished their homes to be, in this universe there is a place for everything and everything is in its place — or will get there sooner or later. So place becomes a fundamental category in Aristotle's treatise in *Physics*. When it has been satisfactorily defined, the orderliness of the whole universe becomes at once apparent, not just to our minds but especially to our mind's eye. Aristotle, as it were, holds up before us the totality of things, properly arranged and put in a glass container for us to look at. He explains in his *Physics* that, as the spheres of the heavens revolve around the motionless earth, "up" and "down" are fixed and forever the same. So, too, what is naturally carried up is light and the heavy is that which is carried downward. *Place* is a fundamental category, and one which presents no difficulty. Things simply are where they are.

In Aristotle's cosmology there is even more regularity than in the marching order of the Brave Old Duke of York's troops. What is up is up and what is down is down. And what is halfway up is either up or down, too. Nothing is left out or left over. Not even man. He is placed comfortably in the middle, definitely down as man, though with godlike powers of intellect lifting him beyond himself.

Aristotle's cosmology formed the basis of the Medieval world view. Only now, instead of a universe kept running by a Prime Mover oblivious of all else except his own complete perfection, there was this same universe watched over by a Prime Mover who was also a Creator having a particular concern about each part of his creation, and especially about his creature, man. The symmetry of the up-and-down cosmos of Aristotle was extended by the addition of heaven, hell and purgatory. We find the whole thing drawn in detail in Dante's *Divine Comedy,* mapped out visually, so that we can follow Dante as he progresses from this *place* to the next *place,* each with its neat boundary after the Aristotelian prescription. Of course, it can only be a comedy, this survey of a universe where nothing is loose or ragged or absurd, and where the degrees of bliss in heaven are balanced by the degrees of pain in hell.

The Medieval world view was broken by the rise of natural science, which threw out the geocentric hypothesis upon which the Aristotelian up-and-down universe had been founded. The sound of the smashing of Aristotle's glass showcase was so loud that we still hear echoes of it four centuries later. What we may perhaps overlook is that the scientific revolution that has transformed our culture has done so by bringing forward its own model of the universe. And this model, though infinitely more complex than Aristotle's, is not at all different from his in intention. The scientific purpose is also to present the universe as a regular arrangement of objects open to our inspection. Nothing is to be left out, not even man himself.

The most obvious difference dividing our scientifically orientated cosmology from the Aristotelian one is that we no longer trust our eyes as fully as Aristotle told us we could. With a motionless earth at the hub of the universe taken away, things are not any more to be put in their place by measuring where they stand in relation to us by means of an absolute up-and-down scale. Scientists have given up trying to provide visual models of the structures of our universe and rely upon mathematics to convey to us the way things are. Eddington used to remind us that the reality of the world, as it reaches us in the form of scientific data, is a series of pointer-readings. It is these pointer-readings which constitute our knowledge of the world, so that we can no longer stand on the naïve assumption that seeing is believing. Yet the difference between the world view of modern science and the world view of Aristotle as it stems from the removal of our earth from the center of the cosmos, and the consequent sophistication of our picture of reality, is not, except literally speaking, a world of difference. We still trust in this world view to give us objective knowledge of the shape of what is there to be seen. We can travel in space now, actually experiencing for the first time release from being tied to the old understanding of an absolute up and down. But we still expect to journey from *here* to *there,* travelling from one place in order to arrive at the next place, knowing where we are going, and plotting the stages of our progress. In fact, when the chips are down, seeing is still believing. We may phrase it abstractly, saying that scientific knowledge proceeds through the verification of hypotheses. In practice this means that we trace the orbit of a planet as yet unknown and then wait for it to appear. Before we can land on the surface of the moon we send a rocket there to tell us what it is like — by sending back pictures, among other things.

Where the more significant difference lies between the modern scientific world view and the Aristotelian is in its view of man. Here the geocentric picture of reality, with its absolute up and down, is a whole human world away from the contemporary relativistic picture. Man for Aristotle, as Martin Buber points out, is always a "he" and not an "I." He is part of the furniture of the cosmos, looked at wholly from without. As much as a weed or a star he has his place in the order of things, a place with definite boundaries defining its shape and size. But, even more significantly, this place has a definite position on the up-and-down scale. Man is in the middle. He is less than a god and more than an animal. The Medieval world view elaborated the picture of man, thus placed objectively at the heart of divine order. Therefore St. Thomas Aquinas looked at man and decided that what obviously sets him apart from the rest of nature is, as Aristotle had noted, his capacity for happiness; but an intellectual happiness, and so rooted in the ultimate reality which intellect discerns: God.

St. Thomas believed that all must agree that God is man's highest good. Therefore the conclusion that man is meant to know God and love Him is the result of a deductive argument. For we can look at man, see his place in the universe, and so establish the meaning of his existence. All this is possible without passing over from cosmology to anthropology. We do not have to bring in our subjective consciousness and to ask what it means to be an "I" facing the world outside us. It is enough to be given the opportunity to look at man who is "he," one of the many objects to be found in the universe, yet having a distinct place, and being unlike anything else because of his precise location in the scheme of things.

When the glass showcase of the Aristotelian universe was shattered, it was this objectively situated piece of reality, man, that was lost. Man suddenly found himself without a home in the universe.

Home is the place that stays put. We know where it is and the district in which it is situated. When we are a long way from home, we may have to stop a stranger and ask for directions. But, once we are back among familiar landmarks, our legs carry us there automatically. We have a key for the door, and, inside, we can sit down without more than a casual glance to see whether our favorite chair has been moved. Above all, we do not have to produce identity papers, proving that we have a right to be there. In the contemporary world, however, it is precisely the search for our identity that becomes imperative. At home, the most grudging welcome we can receive is the indifferent comment, "Oh, it's only him." If we have to ask "Who am I?" the response "Don't you know this is your home?" is utterly bewildering. When an age asks that question it has, in Martin Buber's terms, turned away from a cosmological viewpoint to an anthropological one.

In the modern period, the anthropological question did not have to be asked so long as men were satisfied with the universe mapped out by the experimental sciences. After all, the scientific world view aimed at being no less inclusive than the Aristotelian one had been. Man was still there as a "he" within the totality of the cosmos. The real loss was in the rejection of the Aristotelian notion of man being in a definite place at the heart of things, between the terrestrial and the celestial orders. For the contained and neatly bound Aristotelian place had now given way to space which had no certain boundaries, certainly not in human terms. Already in the seventeenth century the sensitive genius of Blaise Pascal had seized upon the fact of the new loneliness of man. Objectively speaking, we might argue that man is in the middle of the universe, spatially considered, between the world seen by the telescope and the world explored by the microscope. But Pascal saw himself as an "I" set unaccountably in a world which, however great or small, took no account of him. And the freshly discovered magnitude of space moved him not so much for its sheer size as for its lack of relation to the meaning of his existence. What had the observer and the observed in common?

BLAISE PASCAL, *Pensées* (1670), No. 205

When I consider the short duration of my life, swallowed up in the eternity before and after, the little space which I fill, and even can see, engulfed in the infinite immensity of spaces of which I am ignorant, and which know me not, I am frightened, and am astonished at being here rather than there; for there is no reason why here rather than there, why now rather than then. Who has put me here? By whose order and direction have this place and time been allotted to me?

No. 206

The eternal silence of these infinite spaces frightens me.

No. 207

How many kingdoms know us not!

Pascal's question is still being asked in our own day. Martin Heidegger speaks of the "thrown-ness" of existence. Man has been hurled, willy-nilly, into the being which he enjoys or must endure, and life is an exile. Albert Camus sees human experience as experience of the Absurd. Life and meaning exclude each other, for the scientific universe is self-contained.

31

It provides man with space to roam in, but no place where he can be at home. Man can go anywhere, but what is he? What is his highest good? If he shouts his question to the heavens which science knows, no answer comes back from those infinite spaces. So he must ponder the question within his own breast, a lonely "I" parted from the whole observable world of things.

Through the whole of the modern era runs the anxious cry of the individual set over against a scheme of nature in which he finds no home. The world is a split world, divided into a reality divorced from the "I" and the "I" without a relationship to the world which he is forced to believe is the sole known reality. What makes the loss of the Aristotelian cosmology so great a loss is that the religious faith that consoled man, making the human condition bearable, was seen in terms of that world view. Beyond the natural world, yet an extension of it, lay the supernatural world where man found his ultimate meaning. God was the Ground of all, the Source of man's being and his final End. God ruled the created order wisely through His providence, giving man a temporary home before bringing him to his permament dwelling-place. There, in heaven or in hell, man would willingly or unwillingly, according to the quality of his spirit, testify to the wisdom and to the goodness of Him who did all things well and who had made man that he might respond to the Love that had brought him into being. The world of space and time was the theatre of God's glory. And the end of that world was the beginning of man's true fulfilment.

The Loss of the Presence of God

IT IS ALWAYS EXCITING TO PULL DOWN AN OLD BUILDING IN order to build a new one on the same site, if you believe that the old has outlived its usefulness and you have dreams for the future. The smashing of the Aristotelian cosmology and the employment of the scientific method to uncover the secrets of nature was an exhilarating process — and still is. But a price has to be paid for each venture to be independent of the past. It is no wonder that men, finding themselves homeless, should wonder before long whether their present labors were not misguided by their new plans misconceived, and should turn back with nostalgia to the home they had destroyed. Much of the literature of the nineteenth century carries overtones of such a mood. Sometimes, indeed, the homeless "I" complains openly and even bitterly of what it has lost.

MATTHEW ARNOLD, "Dover Beach," 1867

The sea is calm tonight.
The tide is full, the moon lies fair
Upon the straits — on the French coast the light
Gleams and is gone; the cliffs of England stand,
Glimmering and vast, out in the tranquil bay.
Come to the window, sweet is the night air!
Only, from the long line of spray
Where the sea meets the moon-blanched sand,
Listen! you hear the grating roar
Of pebbles which the waves draw back, and fling,
At their return, up the high strand,
Begin, and cease, and then again begin,
With tremulous cadence slow, and bring
The eternal note of sadness in.

Sophocles long ago
Heard it on the Aegean, and it brought
Into his mind the turbid ebb and flow
Of human misery; we
Find also in the sound a thought,
Hearing it by this distant northern sea.

The Sea of Faith
Was once, too, at the full, and round earth's shore
Lay like the folds of a bright girdle furled.
But now I only hear
Its melancholy, long, withdrawing roar,
Retreating, to the breath
Of the night wind, down the vast edges drear
And naked shingles of the world.

Ah, love, let us be true
To one another! for the world, which seems
To lie before us like a land of dreams,
So various, so beautiful, so new,
Hath really neither joy, nor love, nor light,
Nor certitude, nor peace, nor help for pain;
And we are here as on a darkling plain
Swept with confused alarms of struggle and flight,
Where ignorant armies clash by night.

The English vice, they say, is hypocrisy, as the French vice
is pride, and the German vice obedience. One may perhaps
be inclined to wonder why Matthew Arnold should lament
the decline of faith and deny the reality of the external world,
typified by his description of the beach at Dover, without doing
something about it. To him the sound of the retreat of the
healing waters, prophetic of the drought of the Waste Land,
suggests only "a thought." The isolated "I," in an anthropological era, here is mainly taken up with the aesthetic fancy
that it has interesting thoughts. A "darkling plain," for instance,
really is quite an appealing phrase, especially when furnished
with ignorant armies. Of course, an English gentleman would
not *really* get mixed up with uncouth company. We are "here"
only in a metaphorical sense. Struggle and flight are for the
literally minded, not for the literary-minded.

An uncouth German spoke out more bluntly. Friedrich Nietzsche did not lament without passion the passing of the old cosmology, and neither did he deny the reality of the new one. He described what he believed had happened, and said, in the most direct way he could, that the days for pussy-footing were over. Just at the moment the phrase "the death of God" is a rather fashionable one. But it is doubtful whether we are, even now, ready to take at its face value Nietzsche's parable of the Madman.

FRIEDRICH NIETZSCHE, "The Madman" from *Gay Science,* No. 125

Have you ever heard of the madman who on a bright morning lighted a lantern and ran to the market-place calling out unceasingly: "I seek God! I seek God!" — As there were many people standing about who did not believe in God, he caused a great deal of amusement. Why! is he lost? said one. Has he strayed away like a child? said another. Or does he keep himself hidden? Is he afraid of us? Has he taken a sea-voyage? Has he emigrated? — the people cried out laughingly, all in a hubbub. The insane man jumped into their midst and transfixed them with his glances. "Where is God gone?" he called out. "I mean to tell you! We have killed him, — you and I! We are all his murderers! But how have we done it? How were we able to drink up the sea? Who gave us the sponge to wipe away the whole horizon? What did we do when we loosened this earth from its sun? Whither does it now move? Whither do we move? Away from all suns? Do we not dash on unceasingly? Backwards, sideways, forwards, in all directions? Is there still an above and below? Do we not stray, as through infinite nothingness? Does not empty space breathe upon us? Has it not become colder? Does not night come on continually, darker and darker? Shall we not have to light lanterns in the morning? Do we not hear the noise of the grave-diggers who are burying God? Do we not smell the divine putrefaction? — for even gods putrefy! God is dead! God remains dead! And we have killed him! How shall we console ourselves, the most murderous of all murderers? The holiest and the mightiest that the world has hitherto possessed, has bled to death under our knife, — who will wipe the blood from us?

With what water could we cleanse ourselves? What lustrums, what sacred games shall we have to devise? Is not the magnitude of this deed too great for us? Shall we not ourselves have to become Gods, merely to seem worthy of it? There never was a greater event, — and on account of it, all who are born after us belong to a higher history than any history hitherto!" — Here the madman was silent and looked again at his hearers; they also were silent and looked at him in surprise. At last he threw his lantern on the ground, so that it broke in pieces and was extinguished. "I come too early," he then said, "I am not yet at the right time. This prodigious event is still on its way and is travelling, — it has not yet reached men's ears. Lightning and thunder need time, the light of the stars needs time, deeds need time, even after they are done, to be seen and heard. This deed is as yet further from them than the furthest star, — and yet they have done it!" It is further stated that the madman made his way into different churches on the same day, and there intoned his Requiem aeternam deo. When led out and called to account, he always gave the reply: "What are these churches now, if they are not the tombs and monuments of God?"

Yes, Nietzsche's Madman is a very sane individual, really. What he says, in his vehement fashion, is what so many other explorers of the inner world in our anthropological era have been saying to us in one way or another. The human condition, it would appear, is for us a state of existence in a universe where the God whose existence has been assumed for so many centuries has died; or, to speak more accurately, has been killed. And we have done it. We deliberately broke the structure of the old world view and abolished the cosmos which had God for its beginning and its end. And so we are left wondering just who we are who have been able to do this thing. We feel pulled in different directions when we think about ourselves. On the one hand, we have the confidence that we can very well live without God, running our human existence for human purposes. On the other hand, there are our bad dreams, not to mention our waking unhappiness. In Nietzsche's Madman's terms: we must be Gods to have been able to reach out

36

beyond the furthest star in order to kill God; and yet we think it growing colder . . . and darker around us.

The Madman said that it would be a long time until people were ready for his message; he had come too soon. Well, he seems to have been right. For, if the human condition is of the kind he described, we have been more apt to look at the symptoms than to care about carrying through a diagnosis, as he wished us to do. We have known all about the common experience of loneliness, the contemporary problem of the isolation of the "I" and the failure of communication. But we have not necessarily traced back this loneliness of the ego to a consciousness of *missing* the presence of a God in an orderly cosmos, One "in whom all things cohere."

Yet the modern mood is, more often than not, a mood indicating a felt lack; the sense of the loss of God alone accounts for it. So, the world is described, perhaps, as meaningless or absurd. We are hurt by the loss of a Creator who saw that His creation was good because it reflected His own perfection. Again, there is a constantly recurring theme in our literature: that of the man who is pursued and harried for some unknown crime. The classic expression of the theme is in the novels of Kafka; and there is something of Kafka in almost everything that has been written since! There are many variations too, for instance, Albert Camus's rather untypical tale, *The Fall.* Here the teller of the story is a lawyer who styles himself a "judge-penitent" and spends his life confessing his guilt. He knows why he feels guilty (or thinks he does), but, obsessed with the idea that no one is acquitted nowadays, he builds up fantasies around judge-figures and dreams of his own execution. Would this particular theme attract us, were we not fretting because of the absence of an almighty Lawgiver and Judge, whose judgments are both righteous and merciful?

Thus, even if we do not admit that the death of God is our problem, we are haunted by the loneliness we meet with in three forms: absence of Goodness, absence of Eternal Law, and the Abyss of incoherence.

37

W. H. AUDEN: Chorus from *For The Time Being*, III,
stanzas 1, 2, and 3

Alone, alone, about a dreadful wood
Of conscious evil runs a lost mankind,
Dreading to find its Father lest it find
The Goodness it has dreaded is not good:
Alone, alone, about our dreadful wood.

Where is that Law for which we broke our own,
Where now that Justice for which Flesh resigned
Her hereditary right to passion, Mind
His will to absolute power? Gone, Gone.
Where is that Law for which we broke our own?

The Pilgrim Way has led to the Abyss.
Was it to meet such grinning evidence
We left our richly odoured ignorance?
Was the triumphant answer to be this?
The Pilgrim Way has led to the Abyss.

That is Auden again. The time is now 1945, and the poet's
concern is more general, more universal, than it was a decade
earlier. His heroes are still psychologists, only they include
religious psychologists, such as Søren Kierkegaard and Rein-
hold Niebuhr, whose life's work was to produce a Christian
anthropology. Before, Auden sought to uncover the source of
human ills in personal neuroses, inner guilt and hatreds, reflected in man's collective life. His subject matter at this later
stage revolves around the question of the poetic vocation and
human self-understanding in relation to God. He himself looks
hopefully to the Christian affirmation that God has shown
Himself — miraculously — in our world. The Incarnation of
the Son of God is true. So the last verse of his Chorus runs:

We who must die demand a miracle.
How could the Eternal do a temporal act,
The Infinite become a finite fact?
Nothing can save us that is possible:
We who must die demand a miracle.

But what about those who do not look at our world with this
faith in God's self-revelation in Immanuel, the Word Incar-

nate? Here "the death of God" in contemporary culture comes right into the center of the picture — as it did for quite a number of Auden's contemporaries just at that time, incidentally. After the war ended, Jean-Paul Sartre welcomed some foreign journalists with the confident greeting, "Gentlemen, God is dead!" And, in a prison cell in Germany not many months earlier, the heroic theologian Dietrich Bonhoeffer had written to a friend, "God is allowing Himself to be edged out of the world."

"Who gave us the sponge to wipe away the whole horizon?" asks Nietzsche's Madman. "Is there still an above and below?" We have come a long way since Aristotle assured us that we knew, with the whole power of our intellect that grasps reality, where the horizon was, and why the above and below were eternally fixed. The Medieval horizon extended to the supernatural world, and above and below embraced both heaven and hell. But no longer. Lucky tells us the flames of hell now rise to set aflame the blue, still calm of heaven. "Things fall apart; the centre cannot hold; / Mere anarchy is loosed upon the world."

No Easy Hope: No Hopeless Destiny

BUT, THOUGH WE HAVE WAITED, YEATS'S PROPHECY OF A Second Coming hangs in the air with no sign of a fulfilment. If anything has been stirring in Bethlehem, no news of the event has reached Peckham, Fulham and Clapham. The human "I" remains alone in the dreadful wood, without a site on which to build a house.

Here lies the pathos of the human condition: the impossibility of finding any inviolate space where a home may be built and remain standing. Matthew Arnold turned for comfort (as many another has done since) to the hope that there was at least firm ground to be found at the point where two individuals met in human affection. Though hell had invaded heaven, and earth was a battleground where blind forces clashed, yet there was always the sanctuary of the heart. And in this place of peace our loneliness could be overcome. "Ah, love, let us be true/ To one another."

Arnold wished to be a comforter of his fellow-exiles. But, as Auden says, we can be glad that not every writer has been a comforter — and a liar.

William Faulkner's bitter novel *Sanctuary* is perhaps a fitting commentary on Arnold's *credo*. Faulkner shows that love is continually betrayed by self-interest, whether in the sphere of sexual love, family affection or social goodwill. However, it is another writer who has most searchingly probed the claim that love overcomes the essential isolation of the self, and found no substance in it. "There was Proust on the self-regard," so Auden reminds us. And Marcel Proust is one of the influences which Samuel Beckett, too, has acknowledged. Beckett's little monograph on Proust is a penetrating study.

Proust explores human isolation in terms of the self's encounter with time, an encounter which leaves man with the conviction that he is a prisoner and a victim of circumstance. In his time-dominated world, man is alone. His attempts to break out to meet others are futile. Our longing for another kind of existence is constant and passionate, but self-defeating. There is no possibility of reproducing in our lives any miniature replica of heaven, even were we to be content with a lesser calm and a paler blue. Our attempt to love is only a projection of the self-enclosed "I." Beckett picks out statements by Proust that close the door on any optimistic picture of man's wish to reach out in love to others.

> How have we the courage to wish to live, how can we make a movement to preserve ourselves from death, in a world where love is provoked by a lie and consists solely in the need of having our sufferings appeased by whatever being has made us suffer?

> Man is the creature that cannot come forth from himself, who knows others only in himself, and who, if he asserts the contrary, lies.

It is not for nothing that Proust has been described as a literary Sigmund Freud, intent on stripping off the illusions we entertain about ourselves, telling us never to trust our feelings until we have probed them and exposed the insincerities we cherish in our self-esteem.

There is no home to be built, then, in a universe that has abandoned hope of eternity but clings to time. It is pointless to seek to carve out a little niche in the time-structure where, for a few years at least, peace can be found. Proust's message was that, if we trust ourselves to time, we shall be unmade by time. And, Proust believed, we have no other alternative. We are the constructions of Memory and Habit, not, as we vainly imagine, personalities possessing independent worth. So it is quite inconsistent of us to banish an eternal order and cherish the illusion that the temporal order — including the objective reality of the human person — can continue as before, only on a restricted scale. The death of God wipes away the horizon of the world where man lives — entirely, not just to a certain degree.

So to think that the existence or non-existence of God affects our view of heaven and not our experience of earth is not to think at all. The consistent position, rather, is that of Sartre, who insists that the death of God is necessary, because, while there is even the idea of a God in the human mind, man is robbed of his independence. To be himself he must kill God. And the conclusion, too, is consistent. Once God is dead, choice makes man. The idea of humanity is empty, an implicate of the idea of God. By meaningless choosing man establishes his unique identity. And the corollary of *that* is: "Hell is other people." Before Sartre's logic, even Albert Camus's wish to serve humanity by willing to continue a ceaseless and unprofitable battle against the forces that assault man seems noble but a little muddled; while Archibald MacLeish's *J. B.,* a modern-life version of the Job story ending with the God-forsaken J. B. happy that his wife still loves him, is quite unconvincing in its sentimentality. In the twentieth century Robert Frost, as much as anyone, has uncovered, in his unostentatious and muted fashion, the inner despair of isolated man without hope in the world.

ROBERT FROST, "Desert Places" in *A Further Range,* 1936

Snow falling and night falling fast oh fast
In a field I looked into going past,
And the ground almost covered smooth in snow,
But a few weeds and stubble showing last.

The woods around it have it — it is theirs.
All animals are smothered in their lairs.
I am too absent-spirited to count;
The loneliness includes me unawares.

And lonely as it is that loneliness
Will be more lonely ere it will be less —

A blanker whiteness of benighted snow
With no expression, nothing to express.

They cannot scare me with their empty spaces
Between stars — on stars where no human race is.
I have it in me so much nearer home
To scare myself with my own desert places.

Frost has come to the end of the road pointed out by Pascal, where the cold of infinite space has chilled the inner life, and silence descended into the heart, which has "nothing to express." Terror has become normal in Lucky's "abode of stones."

Is there an alternative? To admit that we are homeless, that we live in a period of anthropological thinking and not in a period of cosmological thinking, is at least honest, and may open the way for the long journey through the world to another resting-place, itself destined to crumble away in its turn. This alternative is at least open to the Christian consciousness, as well as to others. "For here we have no continuing city, but we seek one to come," is a theme of the New Testament. No cosmology lasts forever. No house stands for more than a few years.

T. S. ELIOT, "East Coker," the second of the *Four Quartets*, 1944, lines 1 - 13

In my beginning is my end. In succession
Houses rise and fall, crumble, are extended,
Are removed, destroyed, restored, or in their place,
Is an open field, or a factory, or a by-pass.
Old stone to new building, old timber to new fires,
Old fires to ashes, and ashes to the earth
Which is already flesh, fur and faeces,
Bone of man and beast, cornstalk and leaf.
Houses live and die: there is a time for building
And a time for living and for generation
And a time for the wind to break the loosened pane
And to shake the wainscot where the field-mouse trots
And to shake the tattered arras woven with a silent motto.

T. S. Eliot, walking away from the Waste Land, found that the pattern of existence is a complex one, and that its unity may consist of the interplay of composition and dissolution. In his *Four Quartets,* musical form supplies the clue to his argument. To others, however, the universe does not witness as it does to Eliot of a total harmony, for they have not been able to find a resting-place, as he has, in a strongly traditional type of faith. For them, the form of our present existence is hard to grasp — impossible, maybe. But this is the human condition in our day and generation. Bonhoeffer, writing in the dark night of Nazi tyranny, believed that we should not wish to turn back to old securities and more peaceful days, but instead should accept the pains of loneliness as a sign that mankind was being summoned to a new maturity, a "coming of age." As he saw it, we were being called to live without the God we had known — the God of a settled and secure universe. But it was *before God and with Him* that we were to live *as though* the reality of God were not given. And a thinker of another religious outlook, the Jesuit mystic and scientist Pierre Teilhard de Chardin, had a not dissimilar vision of how we were being summoned to faith through looking at the universe through the wholly human perspective of scientific research.

PIERRE TEILHARD DE CHARDIN, from *Le Prêtre* (unpublished), 1918, quoted in *Hymn of the Universe*

In the lowliness of fear and the thrill of danger we carry on the work of completing an element which the mystical body of Christ can draw *only* from us. Thus to our peace is added the exaltation of creating, perilously, an eternal work which will not exist without us. Our trust in God is quickened and made firmer by the passionate eagerness of man to conquer the earth.

Martin Buber speaks of this age, not as the age of the Death of God but as the age of the Eclipse of God. The universe is not dissolved, he argues, when something comes between our eyes and the light. Buber maintains that the world we have chosen is a world of things, an "I-It" world severed from the healing world of the "I-Thou" where man is joined to the God who holds all things together, the world outside us and the

45

personal world we know from within. Having neglected the order where peace is to be found, we find our homelessness unbearable.

Perhaps there is here a reflection of the broken yet penetrating consciousness of Lucky, who tells us that the elements of the world are as stable as ever they were, although we have lost our power to discern them in a rational order, and although society is determined not to hear about them. This contrast between the order and purpose of the natural world and the bewildered purposelessness of the contemporary human consciousness has been captured brilliantly by one of our younger poets, English-born, but choosing to live in American society.

THOM GUNN, "On the Move," 1959
"Man, you gotta Go"

The blue jay scuffling in the bushes follows
Some hidden purpose, and the gust of birds
That spurts across the field, the wheeling swallows,
Have nested in the trees and undergrowth.
Seeking their instinct, or their poise, or both,
One moves with an uncertain violence
Under the dust thrown by a baffled sense
Or the dull thunder of approximate words.

On motorcycles, up the road, they come:
Small, black, as flies hanging in heat, the Boys,
Until the distance throws them forth, their hum
Bulges to thunder held by calf and thigh,
In goggles, donned impersonality,
In gleaming jackets trophied with the dust,
They strap in doubt — by hiding it, robust —
And almost hear a meaning in their noise.

Exact conclusion of their hardiness
Has no shape yet, but from known whereabouts
They ride, direction where the tires press.
They scare a flight of birds across the field:
Much that is natural, to the will must yield.
Men manufacture both machine and soul,
And use what they imperfectly control
To dare a future from the taken routes.

It is a part solution, after all.
One is not necessarily discord
On earth; or damned because, half animal,
One lacks direct instinct, because one wakes
Afloat on movement that divides and breaks.
One joins the movement in a valueless world,
Choosing it, till, both hurler and the hurled,
One moves as well, always toward, toward.

A minute holds them, who have come to go:
The self-defined, astride the created will
They burst away; the towns they travel through
Are home for neither bird nor holiness,
For birds and saints complete their purposes.
At worst, one is in motion; and at best,
Reaching no absolute, in which to rest,
One is always nearer by not keeping still.

Buber suggests that the broken life of our age, which has
forgotten the stability known to nature and to the saint, may be
our present destiny. But it is not inevitable. The future lies
open.

MARTIN BUBER, from "God and the Spirit of Man" in
Eclipse of God

In our age the I-It relation, gigantically swollen, has
usurped, practically uncontested, the mastery and the rule.
The I of this relation, an I that possesses all, makes all, suc-
ceeds with all, this I that is unable to say Thou, unable to
meet a being essentially, is the lord of the hour. This selfhood that has become omnipotent, with all the It around it,
can naturally acknowledge neither God nor any genuine
absolute which manifests itself to man as of non-human
origin. It steps in between and shuts off from us the light
of heaven.

Such is the nature of this hour. But what of the next?
It is a modern superstition that the character of an age acts
as fate for the next. One lets it prescribe what is possible
to do and hence what is permitted. One surely cannot swim
against the stream, one says. But perhaps one can swim with
a new stream whose source is still hidden? In another image,
the I-Thou relation has gone into the catacombs — who can
say with how much greater power it will step forth! Who

can say when the I-It relation will be directed anew to its assisting place and activity!

Something is taking place in the depths that as yet needs no name. Tomorrow even it may happen that it will be beckoned to from the heights, across the heads of the earthly archons. The eclipse of the light of God is no extinction; even tomorrow that which has stepped in between may give way.

Contemporary man may be coerced from many sides, confused as to his horizons and living uncomfortably in the open without a permanent house where he can feel securely at home. But he is still human, still free to build and to pull down what he has built and start over again. His true freedom cannot be taken away from him — the freedom to turn ever and anew from apathy to faith.